MW01048283

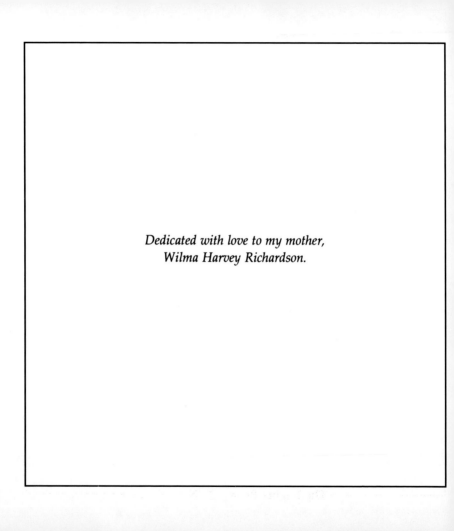

Dedicated with love to my mother,
Wilma Harvey Richardson.

Prayer

by
Patricia Richardson Mattozzi

The Regina Press Ⓜ New York

Published by The Regina Press, Melville, NY 11747

ISBN 088271 488 0

A little thought,
a little word
though I not speak,
I still am heard—

for thoughts of God
ascend His throne
and make His precious
heart their home.

Be with me precious Lord
as my day begins.

Keep me kind and gentle
with all my little friends.

Keep me thankful in my heart
for blessings sent my way.

And may I find still moments
———throughout my day to pray,———

to thank you when it's time to eat;
to say I love you so;

to ask for your help when I'm afraid,
——Dear Lord it's nice to know——

that you can hear me speaking
—no matter where I am,—

for you are my gentle shepherd
and I am your little lamb.

And when it's time to go to sleep
and rest from all my play,

keep me safe throughout the night
while in your arms I lay.

When someone's sick or hurting,
I call upon your name.
Bring them health and healing
and take away their pain.

And if I'm lost or lonely,
no friends or family near,
I ask you to be with me
—to take away my fear.—

And every morning as I rise,
keep me kind and true.
And may my life forever be
a reflection, Lord, of you. *Amen*

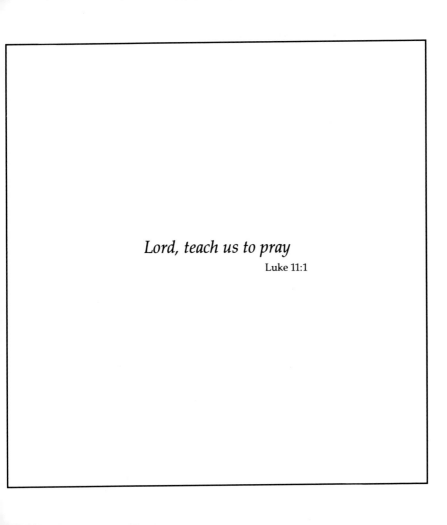

Lord, teach us to pray

Luke 11:1